A small Coffee [illegible] book
for any Southerner visiting
with all our Love.
The Cooks xx

To Sarah on her 30th Birthday
May '07

NORTH YORKSHIRE ONE NINE NINE

NORTH YORKSHIRE ONE NINE NINE

images ∞ richard jemison, nigel whitfield
poetry ∞ chris firth and guest writers

NORTH YORKSHIRE ONE NINE NINE

By Richard Jemison, Chris Firth & Nigel Whitfield

Published by Shutter Books
First published in 2006
ISBN: 0-9551307-3-5
(978-0-9551307-3-1)

Designed by Wendy Jemison

Guest poets sponsored by the
Arts Council England

NORTH YORKSHIRE ONE NINE NINE

A FOREWORD BY THE RT HON WILLIAM HAGUE MP

"North Yorkshire One Nine Nine is a wonderful celebration of North Yorkshire through photographs and poetry.

Those of us lucky enough to live in the county know that it is a very special place, and the stunning photographs and poems in this book prove just that. The images epitomize North Yorkshire with the photographers skillfully capturing the very essence of this beautiful county - its quirks, landscapes and atmospheres.

This book will engage all who open it, with these two talented photographers proficiently capturing each moment in time with amazing effect. The pictures are wonderfully diverse, as is our county, and all are arresting in different ways.

This book will appeal to photographers, poets and those who simply love North Yorkshire, but I'm sure it will reach out even further than that - it really is a beautifully crafted piece of work."

William Hague

'for Les Jemison'
(1929-2006)
from Richard

1
image: RJ
poem: CF

2
image: RJ
poem: CF

3
image: NW
poem: CF

4
image: RJ
poem: CF

5
image: RJ
poem: PB

6
image: NW
poem: CF

7
image: NW
poem: SW

8
image: RJ
poem: CF

9
image: RJ
poem: CF

10
image: NW
poem: CF

11
image: RJ
poem: CF

12
image: RJ
poem: CF

13
image: NW
poem: CF

14
image: NW
poem: CF

15
image: RJ
poem: MB

16
image: RJ
poem: CF

17
image: RJ
poem: PB

18
image: RJ
poem: CF

19

image: NW
poem: CF

20

image: RJ
poem: KB

21

image: RJ
poem: PB

22

image: RJ
poem: CF

23

image: RJ
poem: PS

24

image: NW
poem: IT

25

image: NW
poem: CF

26

image: RJ
poem: IP

27

image: RJ
poem: CF

28

image: RJ
poem: SW

29

photograph: RJ
poem: AD

30

photograph: NW
poem: CF

31

image: NW
poem: WJ

32

image: NW
poem: CF

33

image: RJ
poem: JW

34

image: RJ
poem: CF

35

image: NW
poem: IP

36

image: RJ
poem: CF

37

image: NW
poem: CF

38

image: RJ
poem: CF

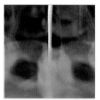

39

image: RJ
poem: CF

40

image: RJ
poem: PM

41

image: NW
poem: CF

42

image: RJ
poem: CF

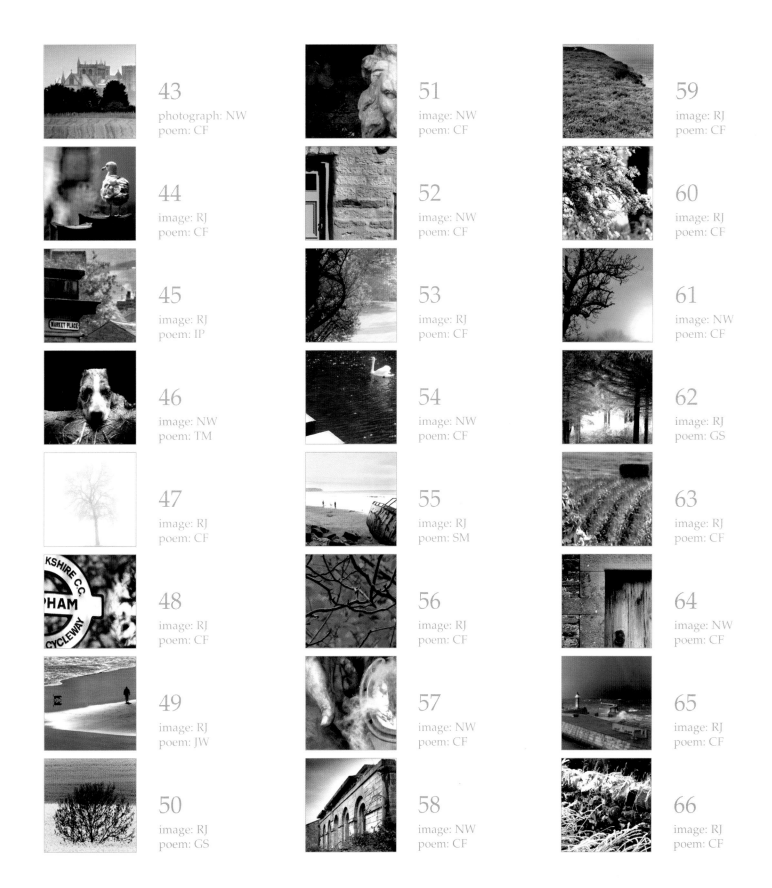

43
photograph: NW
poem: CF

44
image: RJ
poem: CF

45
image: RJ
poem: IP

46
image: NW
poem: TM

47
image: RJ
poem: CF

48
image: RJ
poem: CF

49
image: RJ
poem: JW

50
image: RJ
poem: GS

51
image: NW
poem: CF

52
image: NW
poem: CF

53
image: RJ
poem: CF

54
image: NW
poem: CF

55
image: RJ
poem: SM

56
image: RJ
poem: CF

57
image: NW
poem: CF

58
image: NW
poem: CF

59
image: RJ
poem: CF

60
image: RJ
poem: CF

61
image: NW
poem: CF

62
image: RJ
poem: GS

63
image: RJ
poem: CF

64
image: NW
poem: CF

65
image: RJ
poem: CF

66
image: RJ
poem: CF

Stones

For every stone
There is a charm;
For every grave
A sorrow;
For every gem
A sacred song;
For every jewel
Tomorrow.

Flint holds its fire,
Marble its form,
The sand and lime their walls;

Without the simple stand of stone
A whole world falls.

Flower Collectors

From this rock
So many yellow flowers
Of spring
Clasp
To close a grip on mist.

From our picnic
Daisies, poppies and buttercups
Scatter like dancing stars.
We count and collect them for hours,
Chaining their stems
Beneath a rolling sky.

We wonder
Who made the first daisy chain
Or raised the buttercup beneath a chin?
Chancing children playing beneath the sun
Or wise women dreaming after poppy cures?
Who first presented his love
With a rose?
Whose eyes
Were compared to forget-me-nots?

Clouds pass
As we chain flowers to the day,
Freed from time's chores,
Enjoying idle play.

Scriptorium

In here,
Awake since four with a moonless window,
The shuffling novice is set in his place
In the rack of rows.
Letters are brushed flat,
Pages inset with jewels
And diamond words.

In here,
By the Master's flame
Light is considered.
Daubed pigments are smeared, worried as thin
As a whispering of translucent gold;
Loose hues frozen
Like stained glass in lead loops.

In here,
Can the Maker's mind be captured in frames?
Can the fumes of dreams once grasped be set down
Like furious serpents crammed in a jar?
Can this beauty of life be snapped or snared?

A finger print is sealed upon the sheet;
This frost of breath patterned on ice, complete.

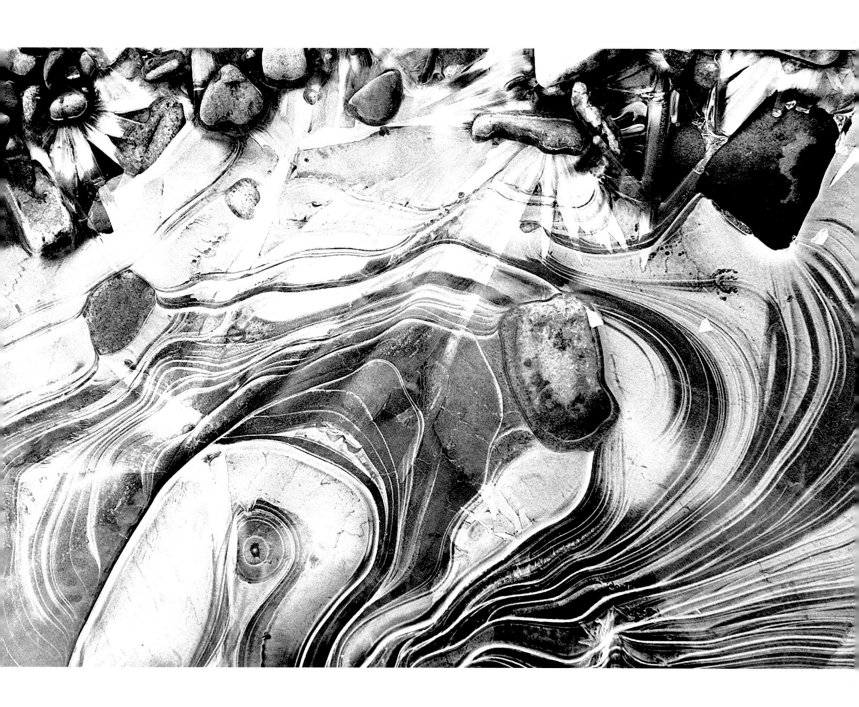

Dragon

A dragon is in the wood
- his breath is smoking white mist to blue sky;
he has set all old summer's trees ablaze.

A dragon is in the wood
- he scatters rubies and gold in hedgerows;
his treasure of jewels is dropped on grass blades.

A dragon is in the wood
- burnished scales spine along the ridge of oaks;
his breath smelts raw fern and furze to pure bronze.

A dragon is in the wood
- his mad-eye fixed there above flaming trees
has the fierce blinding of this morning's sun.

A dragon is in the wood
- his golden wings unfurl the horizon;
He'd be invisible
But for autumn.

Mare

All of a mare. Her sheening belly
barrelled as a covered wagon. Waiting.
Just that one day.
The great weight of a stallion.
His hot breath against her nape.
His wet strangeness, unlike rain.
Something of dew. How it surprises.

Daily, the field
grows used to her heaviness.
Its sweetest grass turns
to a stretch of hardening hooves.
They point to a future
she's ranged before, that timed out
hazy as dandelion seeds. As random.

Against the cooler nettle-patch
her shadow ripens,
until one dawn slithers,
wobbling into foal. Foal,
with a piebald pendulum of head -
upwards, awkward, towards high milk.
His today being all milk.

Tomorrow will be steadier.
His discovery of hoof
and the ground
quickening away from her.
And soon,
How those green perimeters
assert themselves.

Song Stone

Has Man always had this yearning for stone?
Six thousand years ago around here
Humans dragged and ground circles out of rocks.
They pecked lines, cups and rings into boulders;
Their ripples are petrified on the moor,
Riddles that have long lost their gist of song.
Were they trying to compose the beauty
Of this land they had wandered and made home?
Or grinding water signs and sun-moon glyphs
That we read with our own noisy clutter
Of significance and desire to own?

These ciphers set on stone, so instant here
Beneath my gaze and grazing fingertips,
But so distant; a flirtatious teasing
With no link to memory or meaning -
Who made these marks?
What language did they sing?
Here on stone so close, but so far apart.
We can never meet.
We will never know.
Their mystery carries its own secret
Which teases
Like a broken, breeze-snatched reel;
Familiar,
But lost forever on the wind.

Alone

Scored
Or scarred
By what
Is lost
In time
Or time
Itself
It stands
Alone.
Tall-dark
The fashioned
Rock sweeps
Groundward
Like a robe
Of watercut
Channels
Caught
Forever
In a moment.
Tower
Without window
Arrow
Without bow
Pillar
Without statue
Tall stone
With a secret.

Moral of Bees

Summer's surfeit and budding sweet success
Drips in flowers and dips on fruiting trees;
Collecting golden nectar of sunlight
Hum industrious drones of honey bees.

Spittle of light is banked in safe wax cells
As future nourishment - sealed sustenance;
Bee-loyalty to kith and kind, and hive
Is mapped in their spin of homecoming dance.

As combs are harvested by human hands
Bee rage to sting is calmed through smoke and care;
Best beekeepers love and nurture their hives;
Investment which returns a sweetened share.

Enjoy these profits of the honey bees;
When they are spent
There'll be no fruiting trees.

Trap

Winter is preying on my mind.
Her snares are everywhere.
Her arrows of frozen stars rain down
Piercing the blue night.
She scythes through sickly yellow skies,
Blading down grass stalks and seared leaves.
She glances in the smoky eye of the old man
Drinking tensely in the bar,
Counting out his coins,
Counting down his given days.
Her finger blades tap on the spines
Of those hunches wreathing breath fumes
In the frozen streets.
Her invisible spear has jabbed
Right through the heart
Of the blackbird we found stone-dead
In the yard this morning.
Like a mad cat
Her jaws are wound
Wide open for the savage snap.
There is no erotic delicacy
In that death-stroke
Of her fingertips upon tensed skin.
Winter is a hunter;
The fine strands of her days
Are cruel traps.

Before the Storming Moon

Who doesn't love it
When winter's silver rags of clouds
Shred in race
Across gaps of blue starlight
And over the face
Of the shocked white moon?

Who doesn't stand there,
Snatching back breath
From the slap of wind,
Rooted in exhilaration
At those rainbow edges of the clouds?

Who doesn't feel the pull
And the plummet;
The urge to over leap the endless edge
And fly
Wide stretched,
Wind-shocked
Like a flaming bird,
Spiralling
Into the bosom
Of annihilation?

I come with power
And a frightening fly.
After dark
You might not know me at all
But you may well drink ale in me
When I am Black or White.
I have a hobby
And work with clothes
As well as shoes.
Mistake my same sound with a spell
And I'll give you a rasping throat.
Although I can be wooden
I am always ahead in, and after, the race.

I am a ...?

The White Rose

Without the worm, a rose in perfect bloom,
White petals spiral on the summer's blue,
Grown in a sacred space two thousand years,
Seldom is such beauty so ever true.

The spilled blood of our warring ancestors
Stains deep into the soil of this broad shire,
But pure petals resist all wrack and storm -
This rose was singed, not scotched, by raiding fire.

The roots of rose run deep through ironstone,
The stem protected with the hook of thorn;
The leaves unfurl like flags to state a Truth:
Within this rose we're grateful we were born.

Of course, some buds must fall in dark time's rain;
If you'll stand by the rose, they'll bloom again.

Clockwork

If you could reweave and wear again
The golden cloak of youth,
Unlock the relentless
Wind of time,
Out-speed the smears of light
To remove decaying form
Or fix the atom's wheels
To freeze the flux,
Would you?

Would you seize and cease the sea's rhythmic shift
To prolong your summer upon this shore?

Would you snatch the breath of your own offspring
To inherit their spell beneath the sun?

Would you grind the galaxies to a halt
Just to outstrip the bones of your own dust?

Or ride the wheels and swings of life
Until you're unsprung
Like a clock
That's marked right for the nature of its day?

The Sunlit Road

Here upon the sunlit road
The time is ripe;
Sunshine slants shadows
Just so
Upon rusting iron
And mossy stone.

Here among the ruins
The time is now;
A nagging tide has come
Where foam froths its whisper
Through slow skittering shingle
And casts up debris along the shore.

Here along the strand
The time has passed.
A single yellowed leaf blows by,
Back toward the sunlit road.
This is the first leaf
Of so many that will pass us here
Upon the sunlit road.

Distance

To think our retina can frame such distance!
One stretch of cloud above, others lie low,
Air made not just visible but brilliant,
Sharing dip and valley with recent snow -

As if adrift between different heavens,
See moors unmoored, terra turn infirma;
Scaling crests, massed along horizons
Near and aft, stark trees ache for their Summer -

Landfalls beyond this black; this white on white,
A continent of greens and indigo -
At the silence's edge a warm murmur -
Chill monochromes harbouring second sight.

Alchemists

are at work today

Hammering a new universe
out of the blasted scraps of stars

Welding a fistful of sun-bones
to veins and skins of new species

Soldering flux to hard wire brains
and ignite supernova minds

Sparking raw nerves to meld a sense
that perceives with intelligence

Polishing gold to fuse eyesight
that prises open day from night

Transmuting light of thought to clay -
The miracle
of alchemy.

Valley

Today this valley has walked through me.
My banks are lined with firm glossy heads of fern,
Uncurling, spreading wide their palms
To shade a galaxy of flowers.
Sorrel, you say, and Columbine. Perhaps,
But words slip earthbound down their stems.

Morning silvers the tongues of birds.
Music, like confetti, flutters through the treetops
And rests in my damp undergrowth, singing there.
I become a bride, veiled in an heirloom
Of embroidery. My satin shoes
Leave only the slightest bruise on your green flesh.

Valley, we are spread consummate. Your dappled thighs
Move against my dappled thighs. Part them.
I taste your mossy mouth, your lush breath
Sweeter than the stars, the salt
In your running streams. Here, in this clearing
Your stones have opened their hearts to me.

Our laughter has built nests.

One and One is Three

If there is a mathematic of Love,
A secret number sketching God's own face,
A formula to shape tiger and dove,
Then you equate to that by divine grace.

You move with feline guile, but never prowl,
Your looks are fair or golden, never foul;
Your tender warmth is fused with power to feel
The pain of others, some of whom you heal.

Your sacrifice cannot be understood -
You chose me to squander your greenest youth.
My debt for waste never can be made good;
My side is wounded with that deepest truth.

Our spiral lives will ever intertwine,
Our interplay a sum that is divine.

Look - I'm right there
In your frowning face
And I'm right here, right now
In your eyes that are reading this.
There in your hands
I'll bring you a head
And a life.
If you can't walk straight on with me
You could be worse for wear,
And speaking of wearing
I dance with white and washing
In the road and on the breeze.
Some draw beneath me
For completion,
Slipping me slenderly
Between their love and hatred.
If you cross me
You'll be finished,
Or have gone just too far.

I am a ...?

Walk-about

Start here by the morning pool:
Scatters of white air bubble the rocks,
Tumble the ledges to depths
And dark excitements of water.

The shallows:
Minnows flick the egg-smooth pebbles
Frightened for the blink of an eye
By the kingfisher's blue and hungry stab.

Muddy prints by the cresses:
Fox and deer have drunk here,
Sidling cracked limestone slopes
Where larch and hazel cling.

Sudden light after high woods:
A hawk hangs on the sun,
Shadows trace the veins of ancient fields
Where rabbits scrape tooled flints.

The folding skyline:
Heaped moorland carries grave mounds
Grassed where once their stones gleamed white
Above huts where rocks now gather like sheep.

Birth of water:
Rainbows drip from sphagnum moss,
Mingle, ease away earth's skin,
Salve its stone bones then bounce rock to rock
Down to the evening pool
And a deer sipping.

Strayed Sheep

Close, so close,
Raising the tall window
I could have reached down
To touch their black heads.
One carried a burr at its shoulder,
A badge from across the field.
All flowed together, separate and one.
That instinct, that purpose,
To follow a hedge, a cinder track,
A gap or break in a wall,
A whim.
This is sheep.
This is centuries of sheep.
Tight ammonite horns
Tilt them down to the grass,
Busy with day.
Up the valley I see sun
Slipping into some fields
But here snow starts to fall
Down on the flagstones,
Down on the pens,
Down through the fleece of sheep
As they stand by the pump
Chewing the chain for its smack of salt,
Their yellow eyes not seeing snow
But a changing day.

Now they are drifting away.

Boundaries

The boundaries of this shire run wide,
Edging a harsh sea,
Brushing rims of northern mountains,
Bristling the petal edge of the red rose.

The boundaries of this shire push high,
Rearing up fierce winter Pennines
Pressing stern farm houses
Upon brittle-bright winter stars.

The boundaries of this shire run low,
Bruised land soiled with the blood of ancestors;
Great hearts who led the ways
Have passed through with triumphant legacies.

The boundaries of this shire run deep,
Deep through our veins, deep in our bones;
They shape our thoughts and minds, and what we say;
They root us in the games we choose to play.

At Staithes

Night sea hums outside the breakwater.
Overhead, in summer sky
Is a field of gulls that thins and thins.
Most scavengers have settled
Like ornaments set on terracotta,
In turn, accepting dark's long call for silence.

Later, from the slipway.
A harbour light glimmers disordered sands
Then sends a beam glancing off the inlet.
Clandestine, the sea moves landward
Lifting moored boats until they float
Above their image of wooden bow and hull,
Doubling the chances of a good catch.

Now footsteps of fishermen sound through
Cobbled passages, down zigzagged hill-stairs.
White-washed houses tremble.

Reversing the Light

Moors in winter, old bracken
silvering;
grey rainbows.

Sheep
are boulders covered
in hanks of lichen,
thin legs,
sticks of charcoal
sketching a drained landscape.

A scene
for those who love
chalk and pencil drawings,
etchings in inks;

Aware
the world is
an ancient chemistry of ghosts.

Mountain Stream

The slow, solid pulsing of northern hills
- hear it on the wind, booming in thunder.

The sinew and the marrow of this land
- see it veined in mines of coal and ironstone.

The subterranean movement of a dream
- taste the explosion of this mountain spring

This blood of living Earth erupts right here
- it is water; pure water,
Hard by this wall,
Liquid rooted in the crag's hidden ribs.

Marine Drive

This is no place to park your car
In out-of-season darkness near the rail.
Last summer couples lingered near here
To watch the all-night anglers

Casting deep, each hunched and silent figure
Helmeted with light. By now you
Will be shivering, turning dark and wary eyes
To what you think must be the beams

Of a far lighthouse, almost glimpsed.
Whistle and I will not come
Across the miles to talk with you again.
It's not my shadow - stooping, indistinct -

Pursues you down the long, uneven shore.
You'll find me somewhere out of reach:
Motionless, caught in the glare
Of headlights, searching a way home.

Garden

Between raw sunshine and frosted shadow
Slips a rooted dancer of lush, green love.

All gardeners know that they conspire
in the most miraculous of secrets.

Between chucked seed and rampant, scented bloom
Slips the lost chance, with nurtured intention.

Gardeners grow to love even the slug
and balk from crushing its soft, horned amber.

Between Nature and our human senses
Slip interfaces of mind-knit life forms.

The gardener knows
The gardening's finished
When nothing left
Can be diminished.

Silverwhite

Silverwhite spectral mist
Or sacred old stone hillfog,
These hills hail from the cloud like
Heads of old gods.

Gunmetal battlesky lowering
Above the icy frosting
Of contoured earthwave.
The smoke of hill's breath

Shadowblacks horizonline
Sharp against the softness
Of mist veils. Chiffon shimmer,
Kissing the heads of old horned gods.

Tree Circle

See how those trees stand like a structured henge,
A holy place of proud significance,
The tall trunks clustered in an ordered ring,
A high point in the rolling landscape, yet
Surely too young, too beautiful for that?
It's only a coppice someone planted once
Without a thought of rites or solstices,
For the delight of those as yet unborn,
For you and me to see and to enjoy.

No Anger Now

Thirst for forgiveness
And remember -
The roots of a tree
Cast no shadow.

All vengeance
Is futile. It is biting
At the trunk of an oak;
It is kicking at a stone
In the foundations of a tower.

Bitterness
Is wasted. It is spitting
Upon a barren earth
That will grow nothing
In its salted dust.

One day
The righteous axe will fall;
One day
The true fire will scorch;
One day
The final storm
Will unfurl its golden flags and banners
Upon the headlands.
Until then
Let go. Stay pure. Live well
Each day.

Moths

In an instant that incessant tug
Draws her along leafier glades.
Memory's silken skein unravels,
Tangling, mazing
Never following the same path
Yet always pulling toward that same space,
Of heat hazed blur and sensual cacophony.
Exotic beauty, floating, dancing
From temptation to temptation,
Captivating as flame to moth.

He watches from his distance.
Eyes brim full of lust, of desire,
Promising his world for nights of spice laden passion.

In an instant the torrent of consciousness
Floods in and fingers catch
Frantic as fragile thread strains,
Strickening, strangling,
Extinguishing all warmth.
She is drowning in the chilled gloom of that closing room.

He watches from a distance.
Eyes brim full of shame and regret;
Would promise the world for days of innocent freedom.

Each dances still to the tune of the flame.

Graffiti

When I look at Arabic I see sunlight
dancing upon calm water.

When I look at English I see a railway line
Running headlong into the frantic city's heart.

When I look at Arabic I see a flock of birds like smoke
just taken off on flight to a distant shore.

When I look at English I see rows of buildings
With barely any space to move or breathe between.

When I look at Arabic I see sparking Mayflies
carve zigzag jubilations upon a fading, lilac twilight.

When I look at English I see iron forged links
Which make a mind-enslaving chain of fragile thought.

Yet I am English. I am so English. I love my homeland.

Some say that life without Love is an empty carriage.
Allah Akbar! Jesus Christ! God Almighty!
Can't we just let all our Gods be Great?
Life is all One, or it is a Nothing.
All writing is just graffiti to God.
It is simple why we should all know peace.
There was no need for me to write this down.

Patchwork

Cross hatched colour,
A spectrum reinvented:
Quilted green in
Cloth which no sun can fade,
Greyed only by the moving shadows
Of a racing sky,
Unfrayed
Despite the crumbling stitches
In ancient thread
Laced by vanished hands,
Weaving with untrained symmetry
This blanket for the rolling hills.

Spring Kiss Prayer

Her beauty is everywhere today:
The arching of a raven's midnight wing;
The fusing of green flames upon the bough;
The coiling of snail's shell and silver trail;
The uncurling to white sky of our breath.
Her song whispers like a rainbow mantra,
Teasing through the grass and quick winding brook.
Her soft purring of love pervades the heath.

I see her in your eye -
Your eye, my love;
That drive within which does not shrink at death;
A mothering force which meets all threats full-on
And into new life milks a feeding breath.

I glimpse her brightness in pearled veils of rain
That dances as spark-teasing sustenance;
She's in this slow and yearning kiss we share;
In this long, living love
That is my prayer.

A Version of the North

This is the north we're walking in
Where everything was taken
And nothing was returned.
These are the hills that separate
Your thinking heart from mine.
Down in the valley
A sense that something might begin
Is swallowed by its element
As if a lesser god had tried
To get it right and failed;
A quality of light we can't define.
The ruined farmhouse represents
A series of false starts -
Its scroll edged windows
Opening out, its broken rafters
Splintering the sky.
We share the one predicament
With more to be decided
Than the simple choice
Of staying with the high ground
Or the slow descent
Through dim and rainy stages
To the low. Tonight
I'm here, unable to secure
A constant version of the north.
And if love is the answer
Then the answer's in the wine
With which I trace the route we took
In arabesques along a naked spine.

Crow Ghosts

Crude rooks are everywhere;
Their flighting wings fan fingertips
That grasp in the last shreds of light.
From a raw, fist clenched sky
These thieves of life pilfer the day.
They scrape it in crawing zigzags
To withered silhouettes of elms
Where pale murders of crowlets dwell -
Crow ghosts, who never grew beyond the nest;
Naked and grey, for all colour they thirst.

This creak of ghosts
Dredges the yolk of sun,
Draining day's sludge,
Drawing cruel winter on.

Summer Love Song

I love this land,
The breathless curves of her,
The smooth horizons of her skin,
The breeze of sighs at my sight's stroking,
The tender, melting power of delicate melding,
The searching lips of rain.

I love the harebell tremble of the loaded sky,
The engine of power pulsing beneath appearances;
The thundering release in mad lightning and hailstone storm,
The glowing growth of green cascading down all surfaces,
The gentle afterglow about an earth relieved by bolts of rain.

There can be no resting
When we are coiled here
Like a wound up spring.
While I am alive
I will love her;
I'll love this land
And sing.

Snow Bird

Snowflakes dust,
A universe of stars
Floating from night's silence,
Downing a swan's wing along the headland.

The white horizons are feathered clean.
The abbey ruins brush like scrubbed bones on bright sky.

Out in the little world
There is the ice-chaos
Of closed roads;
Children are thrilled right through
With the quiet absence of engines.

On some slopes
Families sledge pleasure
From the delight of crystal water
And gravity.
Hands throb hot-cold.
Voices and laughter always ring cleanly across snow.

For a while
The whole land is layered lamb-pure,
This world transformed
Into a passing bird
Whose white wings beat
A pulse of paradise.

Strands

Alone
We are nothing,
Together
We are strong;
A single word without a tune
Can never weave a song.
A single strand
Won't make a rope,
One rope
Won't rig a boat;
Without the pliant water's lift
No ship will ever float.

In any life, love is the bind
To knot the strongest bond;
All things firm rooted at the source
Will add a strength beyond.

Alone
We are strands,
Together,
Woven rope;
Alone
We will unravel,
Together
We have hope.

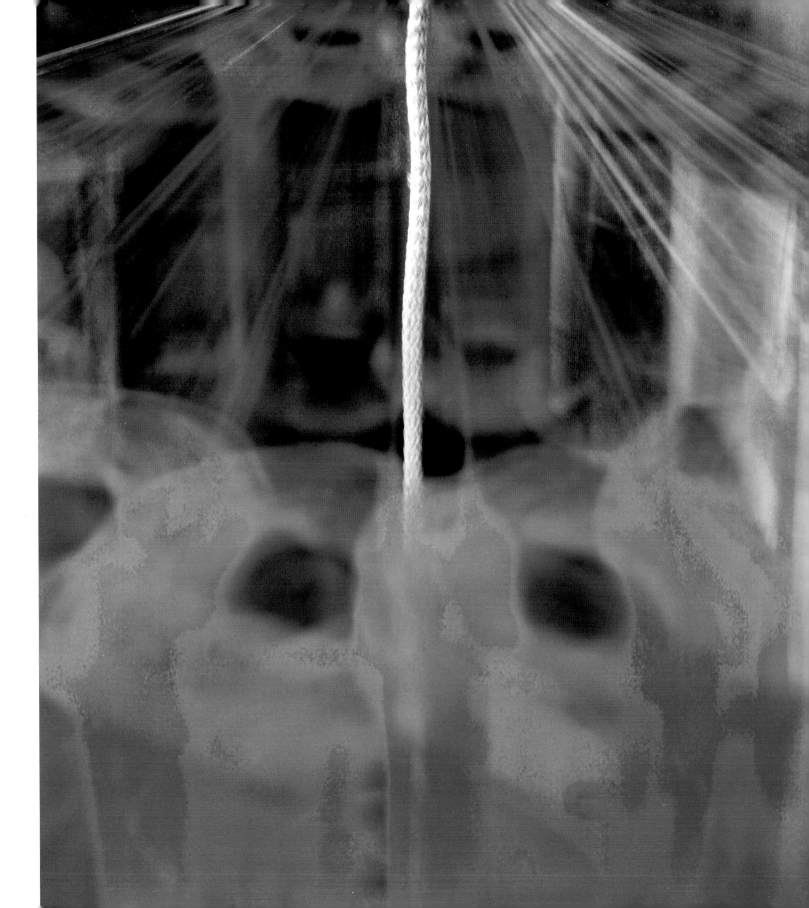

Escape

Lie on the moorland grass
And hear the murmur of the land -
The life sound of a million years.
Encircled by momentous rocks, monumental slabs,
Trail fingers through scattered
Green stalks, tiny leaves,
Minute and unknown flowers.
Hear whispers of their uncurling growth.
Snap of lichen and spiked twig,
A wisp of sheep wool
Recalling memories of bleating lambs,
A small and perfect feather - the huddle of the nest
And whistling winds of flight.
Grit of soil and little, speckled stream-stones -
Sound creaking ice and thundering waters.
Look up at the colossal sky
Freckled mystery of clouds,
Lacy, marbled, heavy or billowing mounds -
Their scudding variations
Echoing faint rhythms of the singing earth.

Become entangled in the harmony.

My first is in wing
But not in prayer,
Then I'm in earth
But not in air;
My next is in sea
As well as in land,
My fourth is in salt
And also in sand;
My fifth is in castle
But not in its moat,
See my end in life's last light
To show kin of stoat.

I am a ...?

Spring Flames

Rain over rain
Sheeting down,
Layer upon layer
Of saturation.
The world is sodden,
Streets sheened to gleam like wet leaves,
Roofs limp as soaked poppy blossom
In a down-poured meadow.

The sky is a flood of grey,
A tent hemming the town in closed horizons,
Damming drenched people
Who hunch beneath wind-flung brollies.

Out in the garden
Cast-out cats are curled to scowling balls
Within precious hollows of bush cover.
The turned soil is a sponge,
Shining darkly like crafted jet.
A black bird watches side-long,
Awaiting signs of the creeping feast.

About the bird
Buds have begun to split and crack.
Soon they'll spring green flames
In the first precocious fling
Of this season's firework display.

Field

This ploughed earth's soil gleams wet and sensual;
Peeled open, she welcomes fingers of rain.
This field, like glass, curves back against the sky;
Spine arched, furrowed, she heaves to take the strain.

That silver sky presses the dark hillside
To bear the weight of summer's golden ghost.
Now cooled, dark soil awaits sun's sparking green,
But before that must whip a crack of frost.

What miracle of thought stirred in silence?
What rippled deep in the velvet cocoon?
Are cycles of life's scattering on Earth
Really tagged to comet and mood of moon?

Rhythm of steamy sleep and waking creeps
Within the very ruttings of the soil:
Cooling -
Dormant -
New life stirring again;
This seed has not been wasted in the spoil.

Glass Work

Today
The sea
Flickers
Like liquid glass.
There is a golden glaze
Over the world, as if to snatch all up
Now and blow it into a molten globe
Seems possible:

Breathe the raw glob to one verdant bubble,
Rotate that glowing sphere to fill the sky
From sun to shore to moor, merge and blend
Land round the horizons of red roofed towns,
Fire-polish edges a luscious trim
Of tidy farms blessed with rich cropping fields,
Fill it with an Eden of blooming flowers,
Scribe blue skies with soaring larks and falcons,
Slip dolphins between lazy, curling waves,
Anneal all faces to cut diamond shine…

This bottled world could be englobed today
When there is a golden glaze about the earth;
When everything seems right and possible
And the sea flickers green
Like liquid glass.

Enclosures

Outside, the paid up world begins to freeze
its assets which are valueless;
But here you lie secure, at ease
with love and what we make of it.

After a day in which the quality of light
dictated everything we did
I let a candle drip itself a shape
around the empty bottle at our feet.

Drystone walls enclose us; the fells
are weighted down with power lines;
And someone somewhere claimed the right
to parcel up the darkness where we sleep

As if the common ground could take
the sealed impression of his signature.
We wake to fresh lucidities;
The frosted window sprouts its new designs.

Mustard

Held low
A candle lights the unseen.
The yellow-eyed dog
Lurks
Behind the wall.

Hear his bark
As he herds his charges.
His reputation
For being 'mustard'
Runs
From the moors,
Across the vale
To the horizon
Where the clouds wait
To be rounded up
In roiling storm.

Maps

The lattice of branches
Pressed on white sky
Is a map of a smouldering world
Which waits to be explored in the hedgerows.

Each juncture, sinew,
And tissue of growth
Is plotted in a bulge of bud
Or crooking node of twig-swell.

With this key
The black night's stars
Unlock potentials of sparks that stir
Beneath the mulched bed of decaying leaves.

The bare tree is a matrix meshed on light,
Marking a route to birth
Between the worlds.

Time Riders

We're here surfing the surface crest of time,
Riding the moment's skin, the curling wave;
This wild, wheeling ocean relentlessly
Head-longing us to our landing
- the grave.

We'll hit the beach and bound upon the shore,
Buzzing, dying to do it all again;
While contemplating ocean from the sands
Through our fingers we'll run each falling grain.

We'll watch the sun go down, the pale moon rise
And wonder on the mysteries of a star;
Around the fire we'll chat and sing our songs
Thereby expressing who we think we are.

With sunrise we'll take to the boards again,
While riding time, repeating this refrain.

Muse

Life's fickle quality lies heavy,
Shifting as it does between moments
Of density and shallowness,
Certainty an illusion dissolved in the instant,
So hard the struggle to retain,
Like footprints in sea washed sand,
Impermanent:
Perfection is never lasting.
Perhaps therein lies its definition,
Something seen at just the right moment
As the light catches all the right aspects
For a second
And is gone.

Yorkshire Spring

He sees the alchemy of curves
Which are the hills and bays.
They sweep the shapes of Yorkshire spring
Down to a soapy sea.
Golden petals spring like shields
Among brown thorny twigs.
He sees the shapes
Transformed
And that is all.

Yorkshire Folk Song

Heart of lion, strong of bone,
Soft as roses, hard as stone
Voice of water, tongue of flame,
Quick to forgive, measured in blame.

We are wrought from Nature,
Right here we'll fall or stand,
First for family, then for shire,
Then for England.

Words of silence, song of bell,
Eye to Heaven, mind to Hell,
Head of diamond, heart of gold,
Nurture the young, care for the old.

We are wrought from Nature,
Right here we'll fall or stand,
First for family, then for shire,
Then for England.

Head of ocean, heart of moor,
Height of mountain, depth of shore,
Warm as sunlight, cool as snow,
Time to dwell here,
Time to go.

Low or high,
If I'm off
You'll hear me
Discordantly.
You'll find me
In the arch
Of stone and
Master crafted
Of ash or maple,
As well as sitting
Between the piano
And the board.
With a hole or a door
You'll need me
To pass through
And when you have me
You'll have found the way
To unlock all this nonsense.

I am a ...?

Valentine Gift

You gave me once a heart of lace;
The star of love shone in your face.
Your love glowed sweet, like June sunshine
To warm our shade in summertime.

I gave you back a heart of light,
Transfused when you were in my sight;
This heart of light, a fragile glass
Through which we watched what came to pass.

What came to pass?
I love you still.
I love you now.
I always will.

Solid Things

All thanks to God
For solid things,
The brick that builds,
The bell that rings,

These stones of paving
Flags beneath my feet,
These bones that hold me
As I pace this street,

The teeth that chew
And grind to feed my skull,
The tunnel wall, bridge strut
And safe ship's hull,

All pathways, stepping
Stones and cobbled tracks
That let us on our way
Then lead us back,

The dust, the soil
The clay, the clod,
For solid things
All thanks to God.

Bittled*

Be still, my world.

Be the grey sea's temper
White wash over me
In waves and waves
Be crash and crawl
Like rock's jagged edges
Smoothed by the salty spray
My voice is silenced
Be crash and crawl
It's in the system
The natural course of decay
No face left in defence

Be still, my world.

*bittled = beaten (NE dialect)

Rose Windows

Words,
Wrought in black curves shall now pass
To twist upon the naked page
Like lead flash around hue-stained glass.

Rose words,
Hemming desire in bars,
Clutching to shape the crafted dance,
Grasp at the living flame of stars.

Windows,
Space hewn in fluted stone,
Webbed and jewelled with history,
Depicting all that might yet come.

Rose windows
Frame a martyr's death,
Illuminate angel and beast
Frozen in the eternal breath.

These panes assist our human tinted sight
To beauty
With the holy gift of light.

The Birth of Sleipnir

Then to Loki, trickster god of Asgard
Not as a wolf, but as a flirting mare,
Was born the wild eight-legged foal
Blessed with the raw stallion strength
Of his wondrous sire, Black Svadilfari.
With double quickness of a lightning flash
And all the grace of Loki as grey mare,
This horse of wolf was birthed in agony
Beneath the blazing furnace of the sun.
When Loki was worked back to his own shape
He called his strange spider-foal
Sleipnir
And was rightfully proud of his offspring.
The genius smith, loyal Volund,
Worked rainbow, moonlight and the cores of stars,
Forging eight imperishable irons,
Sealing each shoe upon the creature's hoofs.
Now mother and father to this shod steed,
Loki was wise to offer Sleipnir
To mighty Odin, The Great All-father.
Odin accepted the fire-wrought gift
And soon he loved his swift and faithful mount.
He rides him still, back and forth across space
From the first crack and spark of creation
To the smoking dusts of all-coming Doom.

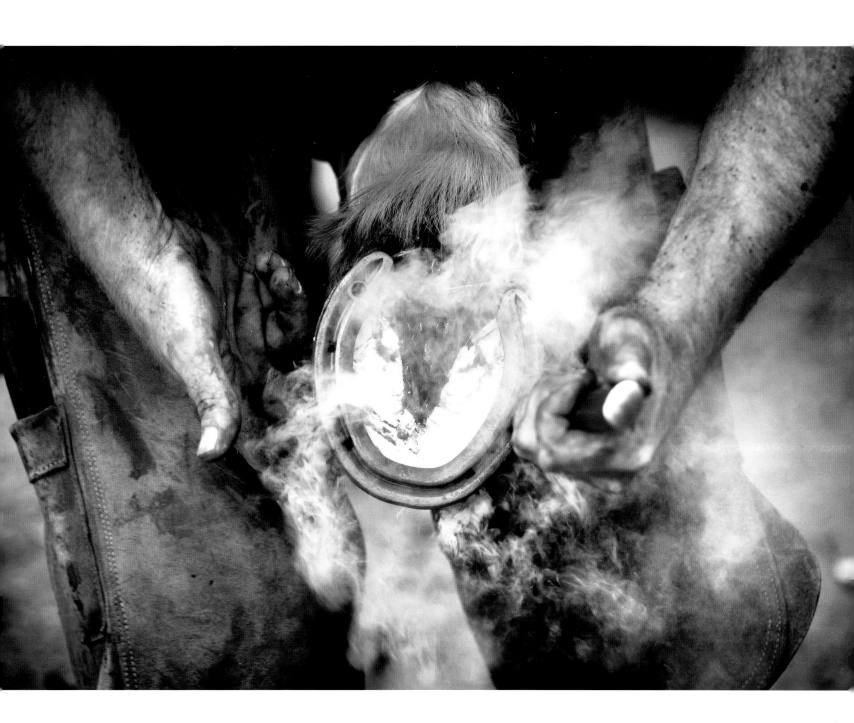

The Sins of Love

Jealousy will not destroy love
But will make of life a whirlpool
Where debris laced water can never run clear.

Lust will not destroy love
But will be a means of measuring pleasure;
A rigged scale that will never weigh portions equally.

Neglect will not destroy love
But will make of life a ruinous garden
Where blighted soil blooms stunted stumps and pale fungi.

Cruelty will not destroy love
But will infuse life with the bitterness of wormwood,
Riddling resentful dreams with ill omens.

Violence will not destroy love
But will crush the tender shoots of hope,
Leading to a life of thorns and broken, bolted doors.

Hatred will not destroy love
But will reflect upon itself like a shattered mirror
With all things seen distorted beyond their meaning.

Love will burn and flame until love exhausts itself.
Then life will be all unravelling,
Like a neat ball of string that falls apart
Into a tangled disorder of knots.

On The Moor Road

Your beautiful, scented hair
Will make fine dust
- this moorland grass is wet,
bejewelled with dew.

Your bones will be
As dry as sticks
- our path ribbons along the coast,
a smolt sea sighs, blue, pearl and silver.

The brightness of your eye
Will be lost like a jewel in an overgrown garden
- a curlew bolts at our approach,
unribbons its startled song upon the sky.

"Shush now," you croon. *"Cheer up!"*

This world is full of a strange brightness.
We hold hands.
Your pulse is the heartbeat of a song bird,
Delicate, certain, calming

And even the grass is in love with us here
As we pass by on this moor road.

Eden

When you are emptied
Then sit by the shore
And wallow in the shanty of the sea.

When you have cast off your coat
Then sit in this meadow
And hear the crooning of the breeze.

When you have forgotten
These twitterings of yourself
Then sit in this earth's garden
And in the moment
Glimpse your birds of Paradise.

Winter Dreaming

In the coiling roots of earth
Winter merely slumbers,
Dreaming of reddened soil
And cool, slinking circles of sun.

She senses the pull of shortening days,
Stirring storms as she rolls over,
Her ragged breath a raw October gale.

She dreams of the garden, bare and rake-scraped.
Her eyes flicker with a glint on the horizon
Of glazed, ploughed fields.

She snaps a yawn, settles again,
Back to sleeping.
But hers is a cat-nap now,
Half broken by the craw of rooks
And a stiffening in the softness of grass blades.

In her dreams
Thorny fingers are flexing.
She thinks she hears frost
In black roots
Cracking.

The Bones of Birds

are in the grass,
Deep between the dew and light,
Caught in knots of perfumed root
Or scattered by the dogs that pass.
One bone beneath my heavy boot,
A minute, pale, hope of flight,
Snaps against the strangled earth:
Broken like a heart, or word:
This delicate white prayer for birth
Into that dream of empty sky,
Heard as a song above the hills.

I'm young and naive,
With innocence and envy.
Once I was the heart
Of the village
And with the wild man
Of the woods.
These days I'm glimpsed
In the face of sickness
And in the illumination
That allows your journey to progress.
I am the very essence
In the rising sap and fuse of spring;
With these fingers I'll ensure
That plants will thrive
And go on living.

I am ...?

Stray Thoughts in Sunlight

Dust motes in sunlight,
Caught in the whim and eddy
Of a passing human breeze -
Is this swirl of variable movement
The same out there
In that mystery
Of the clouds of stars?

Does a spider weave its threads of light
Between the galaxies,
Capturing suns like beads of dew
In the grasses and webs
Of this summer morning?

Is every love and thought
Sapped dry by time?
Every moment
Of pain
And joy
Drained to a loneliness?
Or nourished to a peace
That passes understanding?

Perhaps each star and life is just a door
And when we step through…

Enchantress

Sit and listen for long enough
To this sea's incessant hissing
And there, it seems, you'll faintly hear
Shushed lullabies of mermaids singing.

The drone of winter ocean pipes
With frail ribbons of chorded strings;
The foam flung from white horses' spuming manes
Froths dances to the reels of violins.

Summer's shingle jangles faint bells
As pebbles rattle out their bars;
Whispers phrase in the ever shifting sands
Like love songs gently strummed upon guitars.

The east wind croons with softened breaths
Of silvered voices at moon-pace,
Quick storms are sprung-plucked like Dagda's war harp,
Wave upon wave beats out the slap of bass.

Even the storm-flung kittiwakes cut in
With shrill thrillings of tightly chorused screams;
Even the hail now striking on the strand
Clacks out soft taps of distant tambourines.

Sparks Frozen

Sparks of hail
Skittering across ice glazed tarmac
Drive a blackbird into the sparse hedgerow.

Its beak once pierced the very yolk of the sun
And is dipped yellow as a daffodil;
Now it dives into the iron soil,
Preying on an earth of buried worms.

The storm frenzy falters; peters; passes;
A drab of faded blue flags on the sky.
And just there on the roadside hedge
A sudden spray of blackthorn bursts
Tiny star-white blossom
As though the seeds of hail exploded here
And left these frozen sparks
As hints of spring.

Contributing writers sponsored by The Arts Council England

Ken Baldwin
Walk-about

Martin Bennett
Distance

Pat Borthwick
Mare
Valley
Strayed Sheep

Anthea Dove
Tree Circle

Wendy Jemison
Moths

Sheree Mack
Bittled

Tony Morris
Mustard

Pamela Morton
Escape

Ian Parks
Marine Drive
A Version of the North
Enclosures

Gareth Spark
Yorkshire Spring
The Bones of Birds

Paul Sutherland
At Staithes

Isobel Thrilling
Reversing the Light

Johanna Whitely
Patchwork
Muse
(Muse is dedicated to the memory of Jeff Muse)

S. V. Wolfland
Alone
Silverwhite

Locations:

1   Kettlewell
2   Clapham
3   Richmond Falls
4   Thorpe Perrow
5   Kilburn 'The White Horse'
6   Brimham Rocks
7   Boroughbridge 'The Devil's Arrows'
8   Dalehouse 'The Beekeeper'
9   Whitby
10 Wensleydale 'Thornton Rust Moor'
11 Middleham 'Racing Silks'
12 My Garden 'Richard'
13 Northallerton 'May Fair'
14 Bainbridge
15 Egton Low Moor
16 Malton
17 North Otterington
18 Whitby
19 Nunnington
20 Pateley Bridge
21 Ribblehead
22 Crakehall
23 Staithes
24 Bilsdale
25 Coverdale
26 Filey
27 West Scrafton
28 Kildale Moor
29 Pinchinthorpe
30 Swaledale
31 Norton Conyers 'Mrs Rochester's Chair'
32 Constable Burton
33 Kirby Hill

34 Keld
35 West Stonesdale
36 Scawton Moor
37 Nappa Scar
38 Freebrough Hill
39 Hawes 'Ropemaker'
40 Kildale Moor
41 West Witton
42 Northallerton
43 Ripon
44 Whitby
45 Settle
46 Crosshills
47 Thrintoft
48 Clapham
49 Scarborough
50 Ravensworth
51 Littlebeck
52 Hawnby
53 Hartforth
54 Studley Roger
55 Whitby
56 Bolton Abbey
57 Boltby
58 Richmond 'Race Course'
59 Claybank
60 Thorpe Perrow
61 Dalton on Tees
62 Gale Bank, Wensley
63 Ainderby Steeple
64 Gammersgill
65 Whitby
66 Wensley

Just over two years ago photographer Richard Jemison and writer Chris Firth embarked on a unique three book project, attempting to capture the obvious, as well as the unexpected, beauty, history and culture of Whitby, North Yorkshire. Using the powerful image of the stone steps that wind up the hill toward Whitby Abbey as a starting point, the project aims to produce 199 original photographs and poems related to Whitby and its surrounding districts. The initial book, 'Whitby One Nine Nine: the first steps', was published in 2005 and plans for the second in the series are currently underway.

"This book has the rare gift of being life enhancing."
Lord Crathorne, Lord Lieutenant of North Yorkshire

"They capture the different moods of the seaside town under changing skies, visitors and seasons."
North East Exclusive Magazine

"This is exactly the kind of beautiful book you need on your coffee table, there to indulge in whenever you get a moment."
The Northern Echo

"A marvellous book. You may never look at Whitby in the same way again."
Life & Times, York Evening Press

WHITBY ONE NINE NINE
richard jemison & chris firth

WHITBY ONE NINE NINE:
the first steps
richard jemison & chris firth
Shutter Books 2005
ISBN: 0-9551307-0-0

Highest photographic quality images can be ordered for framing and display.

Technical and image location information is also available for interested photographers.

For image orders please quote the page number and the title of the poem that is linked to the photograph.

Order details and technical photographic information from:

electraglade@aol.com

or

richjem@aol.com

or visit:

www.jemisonphotographer.co.uk

Riddles:

horse
line
weasel
key
green

WHITBY ONE NINE NINE
richard jemison & chris firth

WHITBY ONE NINE NINE:
a few steps further
richard jemison & chris firth
Shutter Books
Due to be published in 2007